Gretchen Bitterlin
Dennis Johnson
Donna Price
Sylvia Ramirez
**K. Lynn Savage**, Series Editor

# Ventures BASIC
## LITERACY WORKBOOK

with **Linda Mrowicki**

CAMBRIDGE
UNIVERSITY PRESS

CAMBRIDGE UNIVERSITY PRESS
Cambridge, New York, Melbourne, Madrid, Cape Town, Singapore, São Paulo, Delhi

Cambridge University Press
32 Avenue of the Americas, New York, NY 10013–2473, USA

www.cambridge.org
Information on this title: www.cambridge.org/9780521719872

First published 2008
2nd printing 2008

Printed in the United States of America

*A catalog record for this publication is available from the British Library*

ISBN 978-0-521-71982-7 pack consisting of Student's Book and Audio CD
ISBN 978-0-521-71983-4 Workbook
ISBN 978-0-521-71987-2 Literacy Workbook
ISBN 978-0-521-71986-5 pack consisting of Teacher's Edition and Teacher's Toolkit Audio CD / CD-ROM
ISBN 978-0-521-71984-1 CDs (Audio)
ISBN 978-0-521-71985-8 Cassettes

*Art direction, book design, photo research, and layout services:* Adventure House, NYC

# Contents

# Introduction

## What is the *Ventures Literacy Workbook*?

The *Ventures Literacy Workbook* is designed to accompany the *Ventures Basic Student's Book.* This workbook provides reading and writing readiness activities targeted specifically to literacy learners. It takes into account the six main types of students in need of literacy instruction[1]:

1. **preliterate** learners whose first language either has no writing system or has a writing system that is relatively recent and/or not commonly used in daily life. The language of the Hmong of Southeast Asia is an example.

2. **nonliterate** learners whose first language has a writing system that is used in daily life but who have not been schooled in that writing system. Examples include those whose schooling was disrupted because of regional unrest and those from subgroups forbidden by government policy from being schooled.

3. **semiliterate** learners whose first language has a writing system that is used in daily life but whose schooling was either incomplete or unsuccessful. Adult students who left school before completing primary grades are examples.

4. **nonalphabet literate** learners whose first language has a writing system that represents ideas rather than sounds. Chinese is an example.

5. **non-Roman alphabet literate** learners whose first language uses a writing system that has symbols for sounds, but the symbols are not Roman letters. Two of the three Japanese scripts (hiragana and katakana), Russian, and Arabic are examples.

6. **Roman alphabet literate** learners whose first language writing system uses the Roman alphabet but associates certain letters with different sounds than those used in English. Their writing systems may not use all the letters in the English alphabet or may include other letters not used in the English alphabet. French, Italian, and Spanish are examples.

## How is the *Ventures Literacy Workbook* different from the *Ventures Basic Workbook*?

There are two workbooks to accompany the *Ventures Basic Student's Book.* The two workbooks can be used by different groups of students within the same classroom, providing meaningful, appropriate activities for a range of levels in a multilevel teaching situation.

The *Ventures Basic Workbook* provides written activities to reinforce the aural/oral language taught in the Student's Book. It is targeted to students who already possess reading and writing skills and provides reinforcement activities at the same level as the lessons in the Student's Book. The vocabulary and structures in each lesson come from the corresponding lesson in the Student's Book. The *Ventures Basic Workbook* is designed for independent use outside of class, although it can also be used for additional in-class practice.

The *Ventures Literacy Workbook*, in contrast, provides reading and writing readiness activities targeted to literacy students who, for reasons listed above, need to learn and practice the Roman alphabet and focus on learning to read and write individual words and phrases. The letters practiced in each lesson, and the words used to exemplify these letters, are taken from the corresponding lesson in the Student's Book. The *Ventures Literacy Workbook* is designed for in-class use so that literacy students can practice writing with the guidance of teachers and/or classmates with developed literacy skills.

Both workbooks reinforce the themes and language presented in the Student's Book and practiced in class.

The differences between the *Ventures Literacy Workbook* and the *Ventures Basic Workbook* are outlined in the chart on page v.

---

[1] ERIC Brief "Reading and Adult English Language Learners: The Role of the First Language" (Center for Applied Linguistics)

# Differences between the *Literacy Workbook* and the *Basic Workbook*

| Literacy Workbook | Basic Workbook |
|---|---|
| ***Target learners:***<br>• learners whose first language has no traditional writing system (preliterate)<br>• learners not literate or not fully literate in their first language writing system (nonliterate or semiliterate)<br>• learners literate in a first language that uses a non-Roman alphabet or a nonalphabetic writing system (non-Roman alphabet literate or nonalphabet literate)<br>• learners literate in a first language that associates different sounds than English does for some letters in the Roman alphabet, or has more or fewer letters in its alphabet (Roman alphabet literate) | ***Target learners:***<br>• true beginners literate in a first language that has a writing system based on the Roman alphabet |
| ***Goal:***<br>• to develop reading and writing readiness skills | ***Goal:***<br>• to reinforce through written activities the language taught in the Student's Book |
| ***Assumptions:***<br>• students need instruction in the mechanical skills involved in forming letters<br>• students need development in the concept that print represents spoken language<br>• students need instruction in English writing conventions (left to right, on the line) | ***Assumptions:***<br>• students are able to recognize and form capital and lowercase letters in the Roman alphabet<br>• students are able to relate sounds to print<br>• students are able to follow English writing conventions (left to right, on the line) |
| ***Tasks:***<br>• recognize differences between letters<br>• trace and copy letters following stroke order<br>• relate capital letters to lowercase letters<br>• read and copy words and phrases | ***Tasks:***<br>• complete words and phrases in response to written cues<br>• apply higher order thinking skills to written tasks<br>• read and interpret short passages and documents<br>• complete real-life writing tasks |
| ***Setting:***<br>• designed for in-class use with teacher and/or peer guidance<br>• no answer key | ***Setting:***<br>• designed for independent study outside of class<br>• contains answer key |

## How is the *Ventures Literacy Workbook* structured?

In order to address the needs of a variety of literacy learners, the Literacy Workbook has a unique structure. There are two pages for each lesson in the Student's Book, at two different levels of literacy.

☑ ■ The left-hand page, the first for each lesson, is designed for students who need to focus on the individual letters of the Roman alphabet, in both uppercase and lowercase. These are most often students who are preliterate, nonliterate, or semiliterate in their own languages.

■ ☑ The right-hand page, the second for each lesson, is designed for students who need to practice reading, copying, and writing individual words and phrases. These are most often students who are literate in their own language but whose writing system is nonalphabetic or uses a non-Roman alphabet.

Students whose first language writing system uses the Roman alphabet differently than it is used in English can move back and forth between the two pages. For these students, certain letters may represent different sounds than they do in their writing system, and the English alphabet may contain more or fewer letters. When they encounter a letter not in their writing system, they can start with the left-hand page. When the letters are ones they are familiar with, they may do the right-hand page only.

Students already literate in the Roman alphabet may be ready to complete pages in the Basic Workbook in addition to the Literacy Workbook.

## What is the relationship between the left-hand page and the right-hand page?

Depending on their level and situation, students can complete just the left-hand page, just the right-hand page, or both pages in the Literacy Workbook. The key letters and words presented on the left-hand page appear again in a slightly different form on the right-hand page, so that the first page leads into the second. This creates a progression within the lesson for students who opt to complete both pages.

For example, in Unit 1, Lesson A, the pre-, semi-, and nonliterate students learn the block capital letters L, T, and F. At the end of the page, students trace those letters in the words FIRST and LAST. The right-hand page begins with the words FIRST, LAST, and NAME in both block capital letters and lowercase letters. Students

who complete the left-hand side with confidence will be able to move to the right-hand side. Students who begin with the right-hand side but feel less confident or need some remediation (such as reviewing stroke order) can move to the left-hand side and then return to the right-hand side.

The chart on page vii highlights the relationship between the two pages.

## What is the rationale behind the order in which letters are presented?

The *Ventures Literacy Workbook* presents the letters not in alphabetical order, but in a carefully designed sequence. This sequence was determined according to three criteria: (1) the context in the Student's Book, (2) the frequency of the letter's occurrence in English, and (3) the type of strokes used to form the letter (e.g., horizontal and vertical as in E and L, diagonal as in K, circular as in O and e, taller strokes as in b and h, and strokes that go below the line, as in g and y).

Extra practice pages for additional work in forming letters appear in the back of the workbook, presented in the same order as in the lessons. Three low-frequency letters – Xx, Zz, and Qq – are covered in the Extra practice section only.

## How do I use the *Literacy Workbook*?

Use the *Ventures Literacy Workbook* to provide your literacy students with level-appropriate writing activities at any point during a *Ventures* lesson. Pages in the Literacy Workbook can be assigned whenever the majority of the class is engaged in an activity that involves reading and writing at a level that is beyond your literacy students' skills.

Assign either the left-hand page or the right-hand page, depending on each student's literacy level and background, or encourage particular students to try both pages. Be sure to model writing the letters, and watch students closely as they trace and copy letters for the first time to make sure they follow correct stroke order and move from left to right across the page.

Pair your literacy students with other students in the class who have more advanced literacy skills. This promotes community in the classroom and frees you to work with more groups individually.

The *Ventures Literacy Workbook* focuses on the recognition and formation of letters in meaningful contexts. Once learners have developed these skills, you may want to introduce phonics – the connection between letter patterns and the sounds they represent. This is usually done with word families and begins with initial sounds. For example, the word NAME, presented in the first lesson, belongs to the word family –AME. By the end of Unit 1, learners have learned the letters N, L, T, F, C, and G. All of these can be added to –AME to form new words. With flash cards for these letters and a flash card for the word family –AME, you can help students begin to see and use phonics to decode words.

There is no answer key for the *Ventures Literacy Workbook*. All answers are evident on the page. As students complete each page, be sure to check and correct their work.

Additional worksheets for each letter and blank writing grids can be printed from the *Teacher's Toolkit Audio CD / CD-ROM* in the *Ventures Basic Teacher's Edition* for further practice, either in the classroom or as homework.

## Relationship between the Left-hand and Right-hand pages

| ☑ ◼ Left-hand page | ◼ ☑ Right-hand page |
|---|---|
| *Goal:*<br>By the end of the workbook, students will be able to:<br>• form letters<br>• read and copy words and phrases | *Goal:*<br>By the end of the workbook, students will be able to:<br>• read and copy sentences |
| *Target learners:*<br>• learners not fully literate in their first language (preliterate, nonliterate, and semiliterate students) | *Target learners:*<br>• learners literate in their first language (Roman alphabet literate, non-Roman alphabet literate, and nonalphabet literate students) |
| *Focus:*<br>Individual letters<br>• Units 1–2: block capitals<br>• Units 3–5: lowercase letters<br>• Units 5–10: decreased font size, relation between capital and lowercase letters | *Focus:*<br>Words, phrases, and sentences<br>• Units 1–4: words and phrases<br>• Units 5–6: phrases and sentences<br>• Units 7–10: questions and answers |
| *Sequence of activities:*<br>• Read.<br>  Purpose: to provide a focus<br>• Circle the same.<br>  Purpose: to distinguish shapes before writing<br>• Read. Trace. Copy.<br>  Purpose: to develop production skills | *Sequence of activities:*<br>• Read. Copy.<br>  Purpose: to provide a focus<br>• Read. Trace. Circle the same.<br>  Purpose: to develop recognition skills<br>• Read. Trace. Copy.<br>  Purpose: to develop production skills |

## READ. TRACE. COPY.

0   0

1   1

2   2   2   2

3   3   3   3

4   4   4   4   4

## READ. TRACE.

0 0   1 1   2 2   3 3   4 4

## READ. COPY.

0   1   2   3   4

## Read.

0    1    2    3    4

## Count. Trace. Copy.

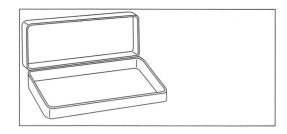

0    0 _____

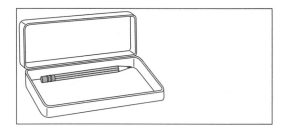

1    1 _____

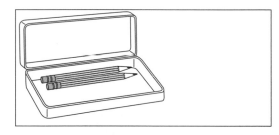

2    2 _____

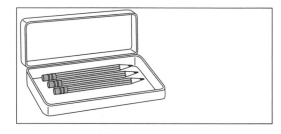

3    3 _____

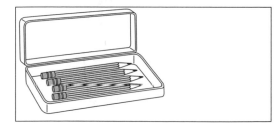

4    4 _____

## Welcome

### READ. TRACE. COPY.

5    5    5    5    5

6    6

7    7    7    7

8    8    8    8

9    9    9    9

### READ. TRACE.

5 5   6 6   7 7   8 8   9 9

### READ. COPY.

5    6    7    8    9

## Read.

5   6   7   8   9

## Count. Trace. Copy.

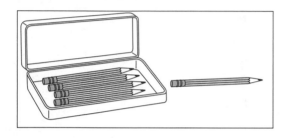

5   5 _____

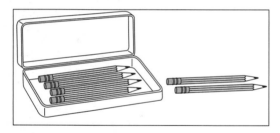

6   6 _____

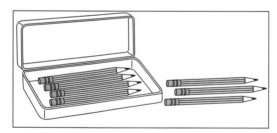

7   7 _____

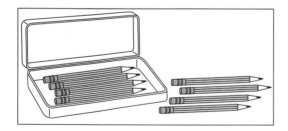

8   8 _____

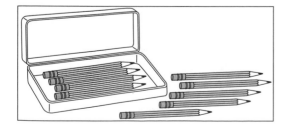

9   9 _____

## CIRCLE THE SAME. L T L F T L

| L | T | L | L | F | T | L |
|---|---|---|---|---|---|---|
| T | F | T | T | T | L | F |
| F | F | T | F | L | T |

## READ. TRACE. COPY.

L    L    L    L

T    T    T    T

F    F    F    F

## TRACE. READ.

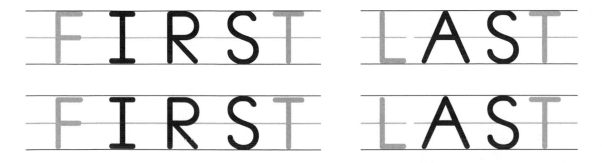

FIRST    LAST

FIRST    LAST

**Lesson A** *Get ready*

## Trace. Read.

FIRST    first

LAST    last

NAME    name

## Read. Trace. Circle the same.    first (first) fist (first) fist

first    first    fist        first        fist

last    last    lass        lass        last

name    man    name        name        man

## Read. Trace. Copy.

first    first

last    last

name    name

## Read. Copy.

first name _____

last name _____

# Lesson B Countries

## CIRCLE THE SAME.  O  Ⓞ Ⓞ  C  C  G

O  O  O  C  C  G

C  G  C  O  C  C

U  O  U  C  U  U

## READ. TRACE. COPY.

O  O

C  C

U  U

## TRACE. READ.

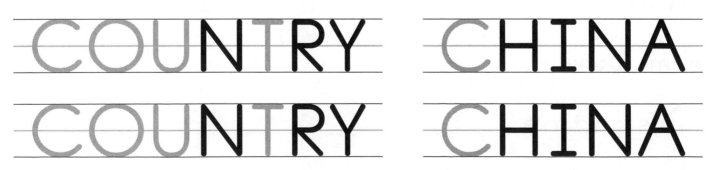

COUNTRY     CHINA

COUNTRY     CHINA

## Lesson B *Countries*

**Trace. Read.**

COUNTRY        country

CHINA        China

UNITED STATES    United States

**Read. Trace. Circle the same.**    country    count    count    (country)

country    count    count    country

China    China    China    Chain

**Read. Trace. Copy.**

the        the

United        United

States        States

**Read. Copy.**

the United States   _____

_____

## Lesson C *What's your name?*

**CIRCLE THE SAME.** I Ⓘ Ⓘ E E H

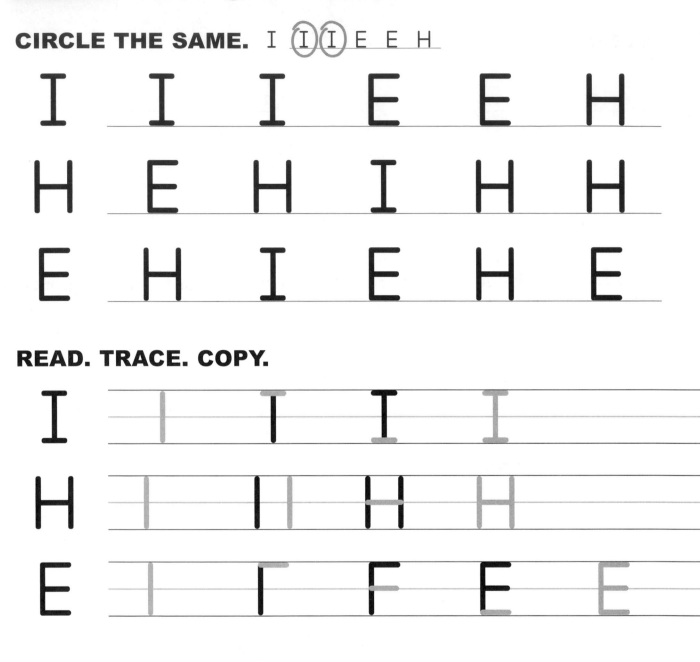

| I | I | I | I | E | E | H |

| H | E | H | I | H | H |

| E | H | I | E | H | E |

**READ. TRACE. COPY.**

I   I   I   I

H   I   H   H

E   I   F   E   E

**TRACE. READ.**

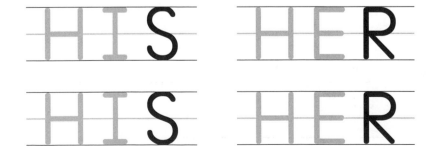

HIS   HER

HIS   HER

## Lesson C  *What's your name?*

**Trace. Read.**

HIS   his

HER   her

**Read. Trace. Circle the same.**   his   is (his) (his) (his) is

his   is   his   his   his   is

her   her   her   her   here   here

**Read. Trace. Copy.**

Registration Form

First name: Hui

Registration Form

Last name: Li

his first name

_____ first name

her last name

_____ last name

## Lesson D *Reading*

**CIRCLE THE SAME.** J L Ⓙ T L Ⓙ

J L J T L J

V V W N V W

G C G G C O

**READ. TRACE. COPY.**

J J J J

V V V

G G G G

**TRACE. READ.**

JUNE NOV. AUG.

JUNE NOV. AUG.

12

# Lesson D Reading

☑

**Read. Trace. Copy.**

| | |
|---|---|
| January | January |
| February | February |
| March | March |
| April | April |
| May | May |
| June | June |
| July | July |
| August | August |
| September | September |
| October | October |
| November | November |
| December | December |

**READ.**

VALLEY ADULT SCHOOL

LAST NAME: LEE

AREA CODE: 212

PHONE NUMBER: 555-7834

**TRACE. READ.**

VALLEY ADULT SCHOOL

LAST NAME: LEE

AREA CODE: 212

PHONE NUMBER: 555-7834

**Trace. Read.**

AREA CODE          area code

PHONE NUMBER      phone number

**Read. Trace. Write.**

| Jeff | Cho |
|------|-----|
| First name | Last name |
| 708 | 555-8421 |
| Area code | Phone number |

First name:    Jeff _____

Last name:    _____

Area code:    _____

Phone number:  _____

## READ.

NAME: JOE LIU
AREA CODE: 209
PHONE NUMBER: 555-7416

## TRACE.

NAME

JOE LIU

AREA CODE

209

PHONE NUMBER

555-7416

**Lesson F** *Another view*

## Read. Trace. Write.

STUDENT ID

First name     Lee
Last name     Loc
Area code     312
Phone number   555-9846

First name     Lee

Loc

312

555-9846

## CIRCLE THE SAME.  A A N N A A

A    A    N    N    A    A

N    N    A    M    M    N

M    A    N    M    A    M

## READ. TRACE. COPY.

A    / ∧ A A A

N    I N N N

M    I N M M

## TRACE. READ.

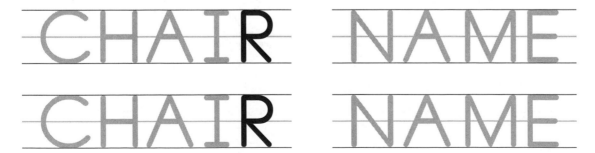

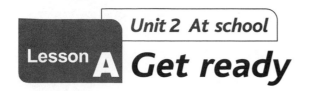

## Lesson A Get ready

**Trace. Read.**

CHAIR     chair

PENCIL     pencil

NAME     name

**Read. Trace. Circle the same.**     chair (chair) char (chair) char

chair     chair     char     chair     char

pencil     pen     pencil     pencil     pen

name     mane     name     name     mane

**Read. Trace. Copy.**

chair     chair

pencil     pencil

name     name

**Read. Copy.**

a pencil _____

a name _____

## Lesson B Classroom objects

**CIRCLE THE SAME.** S (S) Z (S) 8 (S)

S S Z S 8 S

P P B P P R

R B R R P R

**READ. TRACE. COPY.**

S S

P I P P

R I P R R

**TRACE. READ.**

STAPLER RULER

STAPLER RULER

## Lesson B  *Classroom objects*

**Trace. Read.**

STAPLER stapler

RULER ruler

ERASER eraser

**Read. Trace. Circle the same.** stapler (stapler) staple (stapler)

stapler stapler staple stapler

ruler ruler ruler rule

eraser erase eraser eraser

**Read. Trace. Copy.**

stapler stapler

ruler ruler

**Read. Copy.**

a stapler

a ruler

**Lesson C**  *Where's my pencil?*

**CIRCLE THE SAME.**  D ⃝D ⃝D B P ⃝D

D  D  D  B  P  D

B  D  P  B  P  B

**READ. TRACE. COPY.**

D  I  D  D

B  I  P  B  B

**TRACE. READ.**

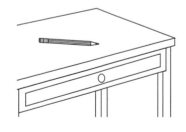  ON THE DESK

  IN THE BOOK

22

# Lesson C  *Where's my pencil?*

## Trace. Read.

IN        in

ON        on

DESK      desk

BOOK      book

## Read. Trace. Circle the same.    on  (on)(on)(on)  son

on        on        on        on        son

in        in        tin       in        in

desk      desk      rest      desk      desk

book      book      book      hook      book

## Read. Trace. Copy.

on the desk      on the desk

in the book      in the book

in the desk      in the desk

## CIRCLE THE SAME. K Ⓚ R B R Ⓚ

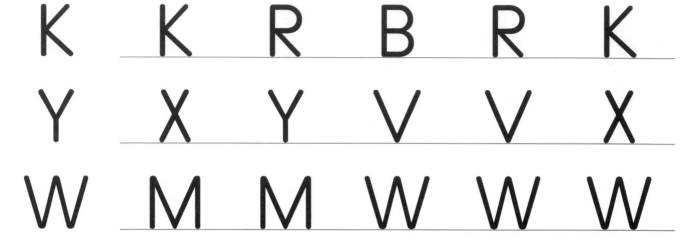

K    K    R    B    R    K

Y    X    Y    V    V    X

W    M    M    W    W    W

## READ. TRACE. COPY.

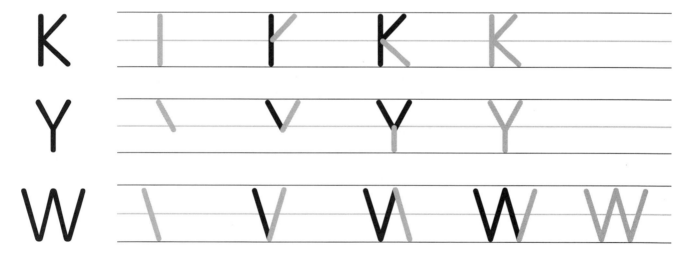

K    |' |' K  K

Y    \  V  Y  Y

W    \  V  V  W  W

## TRACE. READ.

WEEK    DAY

WEEK    DAY

24

#  Lesson D Reading

## Trace. Read.

WEEK   week

DAY    day

## Read. Trace. Copy.

| | |
|---|---|
| week | week |
| day | day |
| Sunday | Sunday |
| Monday | Monday |
| Tuesday | Tuesday |
| Wednesday | Wednesday |
| Thursday | Thursday |
| Friday | Friday |
| Saturday | Saturday |

**READ. CIRCLE THE SAME.**   PEN   PAN (PEN)

# PEN   PAN   PEN

# BOOK LOOK BOOK

**READ. TRACE.**

# PEN   PEN   PEN

# BOOK BOOK BOOK

**TRACE. READ.**

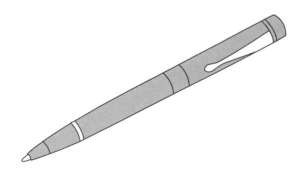

A PEN

A BOOK

**26**

## Read. Trace.

School Supplies
☑ an eraser
☑ a book
☑ a pen
☑ a pencil

## Write.

an eraser

**READ.**

> # SOUTH SIDE ADULT SCHOOL
> ## CLASS: TUESDAY
> ## THURSDAY
> ## YOU NEED: PAPER
> ## A PENCIL

**TRACE. READ.**

TUESDAY

THURSDAY

PAPER

PENCIL

**Read. Trace.**

Kennedy Adult School English Class
Monday  Tuesday  Thursday  Friday
You need
☑ a book
☑ a pen
☑ a pencil
☑ paper

**Write the days.**

Monday _____ _____ _____

**Write the supplies.**

a   book _____

____ _____

____ _____

_____

## CIRCLE THE SAME.  a  o (a) (a) e (a)

a  o  a  a  e  a

e  e  c  e  o  e

r  r  n  r  n  r

## READ. TRACE. WRITE.

a  o  a  a

e  —  e  e

r  ı  r  r

## TRACE. READ.

father   mother

father   mother

**Trace. Read.**

FATHER    father

MOTHER    mother

GRAND    grand

**Read. Trace. Circle the same.** father    farther (father) (father)

father    farther    father    father

mother    mother    other    mother

grand    gland    grand    grand

**Read. Trace. Copy.**

father    father

mother    mother

grand    grand

**Read. Copy.**

grandfather    _____

grandmother    _____

## Lesson B  *Family members*

**CIRCLE THE SAME.**  i (i) l t (i) l

i    i    l    l    t    i    l

c    o    e    e    c    c

u    n    u    v    v    u

**READ. TRACE. COPY.**

i    i    i    i

c    c

u    u    u    u

**TRACE. READ.**

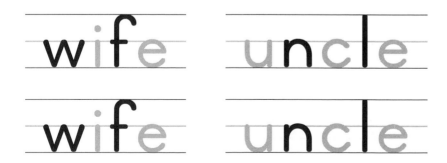

wife    uncle

wife    uncle

## Lesson B  *Family members*

**Trace. Read.**

WIFE        wife

UNCLE       uncle

AUNT        aunt

**Read. Trace. Circle the same.**   wife   life (wife) (wife) life

wife     life        wife       wife        life

uncle    uncle       uncle      unclear     uncle

aunt     aunt        aunt       ant         aunt

**Read. Trace. Copy.**

wife     wife

uncle    uncle

aunt     aunt

**Read. Copy.**

a wife

an uncle

**Lesson C** *Do you have a sister?*

**CIRCLE THE SAME.** d   b  ⓓ  p  ⓓ  b

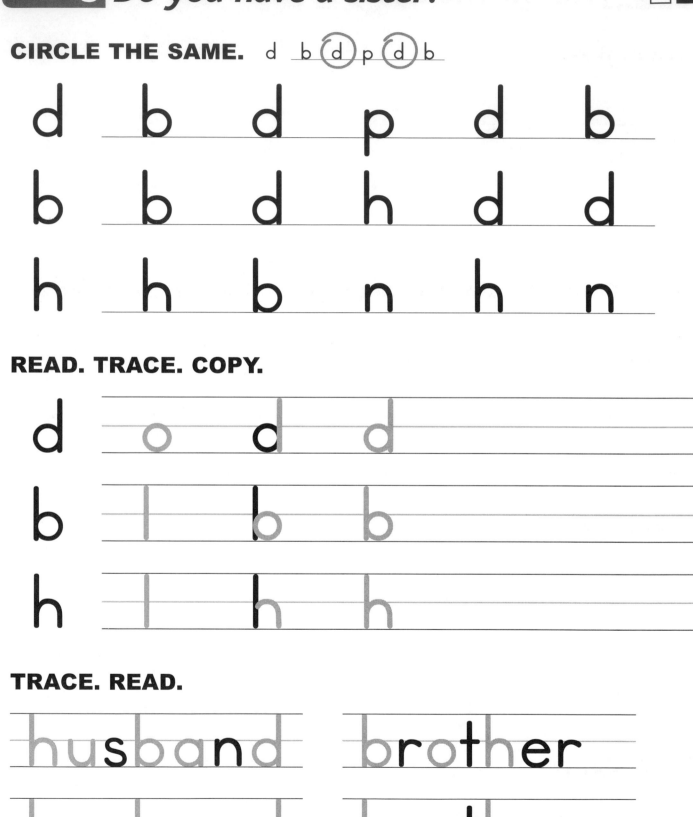

| | | | | | |
|---|---|---|---|---|---|
| d | b | d | p | d | b |
| b | b | d | h | d | d |
| h | h | b | n | h | n |

**READ. TRACE. COPY.**

d   o   d   d

b   b   b

h   h   h

**TRACE. READ.**

husband   brother

husband   brother

## Lesson C  Do you have a sister?

**Trace. Read.**

HUSBAND    husband

DAUGHTER    daughter

BROTHER    brother

**Read. Trace. Circle the same.**   husband    his band (husband)

husband    his band    husband

daughter    daughter    laughter

brother    bother    brother

**Read. Trace. Copy.**

husband    husband

daughter    daughter

brother    brother

**Read. Copy.**

a husband

a brother

## Lesson D Reading

**READ. CIRCLE THE SAME.**  birth (birth) berth (birth)

birth    birth    berth    birth

day    bay    bay    day

**READ. TRACE.**

birth    birth    birth    birth

day    day    day    day

**TRACE. READ.**

birthday    birthday

## Lesson **D** *Reading*  ☑

**Trace. Read.**

BIRTHDAY    birthday

GIRL        girl

BOY         boy

**Read. Trace. Circle the same.**    birthday    day    day    (birthday)

birthday    day    day    birthday

girl        grill    grill    girl

boy         boy    bay    boy

**Read. Trace. Copy.**

birthday    birthday

girl        girl

boy         boy

**Read. Copy.**

girl and boy  _____

**37**

**TRACE. READ.**

husband

wife

**READ. TRACE.**

husband husband

wife wife

**TRACE. READ.**

husband and wife

38

# Lesson E  *Writing*

## Trace. Copy.

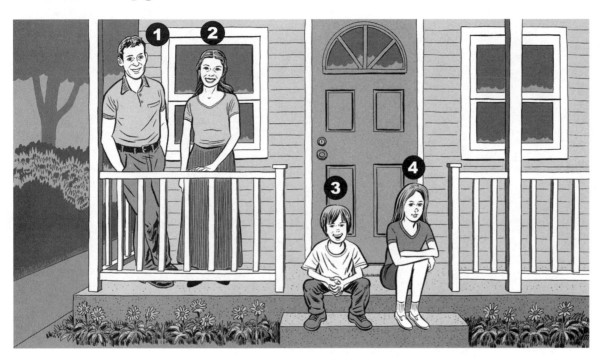

1. husband _____

2. wife _____

3. brother _____

4. sister _____

## Read. Copy.

brother and sister _____

husband and wife _____

**TRACE.**

1. **mother**

2. **father**

3. **daughter**

**TRACE. READ.**

**mother and father**

## Lesson F Another view

**Trace. Copy.**

1. grandmother _____

2. grandfather _____

3. mother _____

4. father _____

5. daughter _____

**Read. Copy.**

grandmother and grandfather

_____

## CIRCLE THE SAME.   t   _f   l_ (t) f (t)

t   f   l   t   f   t

f   t   f   t   f   f

p   p   g   p   q   p

**READ. TRACE. COPY.**

t   l   t   t

f   f   f   f

p   t   p   p

**TRACE. READ.**

patient   office

patient   office

## Trace. Read.

PATIENT   patient

OFFICE   office

DOCTOR   doctor

## Read. Trace. Circle the same.   patient (patient) (patient) patent

patient   patient   patient   patent

office   office   offer   office

doctor   dock   doctor   doctor

## Read. Trace. Copy.

patient   patient

office   office

doctor   doctor

## Read. Copy.

patient   _____

office   _____

## Lesson B Parts of the body

**CIRCLE THE SAME.** o o c o c o

o    o    c    o    c    o

n    m    n    n    m    n

m    m    m    n    n    m

**READ. TRACE. COPY.**

o    o

n    n    n

m    n    m    m

**TRACE. READ.**

stomach    hand

stomach    hand

44

Lesson **B** *Parts of the body*

**Trace. Read.**

STOMACH     stomach

HAND        hand

FOOT        foot

ARM         arm

**Read. Trace. Circle the same.**  stomach    storm (stomach) storm

stomach     storm     stomach     storm

hand        head      hand        hand

foot        foot      fool        foot

arm         arm       arm         arms

**Read. Trace. Copy.**

stomach     stomach _____

**Read. Copy.**

my stomach  _____

**45**

## Lesson C  *My feet hurt.*

**CIRCLE THE SAME.**  s    z   s   z   s   z

S    Z    S    Z    S    Z

l    i    l    t    l    l

g    y    j    g    g    y

### READ. TRACE. WRITE.

s    s

l    l

g    o    g    g

### TRACE. READ.

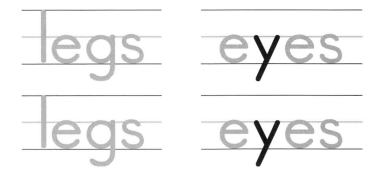

legs    eyes

legs    eyes

46

Lesson **C** *My feet hurt.*

## Trace. Read.

LEGS     legs

EYES     eyes

HANDS    hands

## Read. Trace. Circle the same.  legs  (legs) (legs) (legs)  leg

legs     legs     legs     legs     leg

eyes     eye      eyes     eyes     eyes

hands    hands    hand     hands    hands

## Read. Trace. Copy.

legs     legs

eyes     eyes

hands    hands

## Read. Copy.

2 legs

2 eyes

## READ. CIRCLE THE SAME.  cold  <u>old</u>  (cold)

cold    <u>old   cold</u>

sore    <u>sole   sore</u>

throat  <u>oat   throat</u>

## READ. TRACE. COPY.

cold    cold

sore    sore

throat  throat

## TRACE. READ.

a cold

a sore throat

**Trace. Read.**

SORE THROAT     sore throat

COLD            cold

HEADACHE        headache

**Read. Trace. Copy.**

### a sore throat

a sore throat

### a cold

a cold

### a headache

a headache

## READ. CIRCLE THE SAME. tooth (tooth) teeth

tooth    tooth    teeth

head    head    bead

ache    acne    ache

## READ. TRACE. COPY.

tooth    tooth

head    head

ache    ache

## TRACE. READ.

a toothache

a headache

50

## Read. Trace. Write.

| DOCTOR'S OFFICE | |
|---|---|
| Patient | Reason for visit |
| Carrie | sore throat |
| Linda | stomachache |
| Bud | headache |
| Ali | cold |
| Rae | toothache |

Carrie    sore throat

Linda    _____

Bud    _____

Ali    _____

Rae    _____

## READ.

MEDICINE FOR
- ☑ legs
- ☑ hands
- ☑ feet
- ☑ stomach

## TRACE. READ. COPY.

legs

hands

feet

stomach

# Lesson F  *Another view*

## Read. Trace.

MEDICINE FOR

eyes

legs

hands

stomach

## Write.

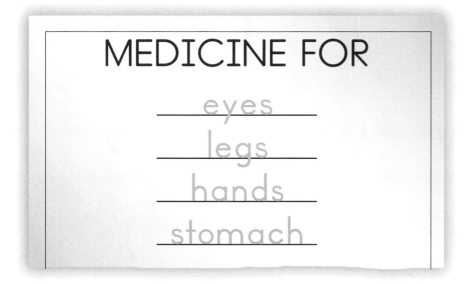

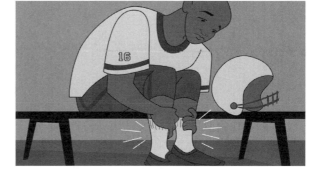

eyes

_____

_____

_____

## CIRCLE THE SAME.  k  h (k)(k) h (k)

k    h    k    k    h    k

w    v    w    w    v    w

y    v    y    y    v    y

## READ. TRACE. COPY.

k    k    k    k    k

w    w    w    w    w

y    y    y

## TRACE. READ.

bank    town    library

bank    town    library

54

## Lesson A *Get ready*

**Trace. Read.**

BANK        bank

TOWN        town

LIBRARY    library

**Read. Trace. Circle the same.**  bank    back  (bank)  back

bank      back          bank          back

town      town          town          down

library   literary      library       library

**Read. Trace. Copy.**

bank      bank

town      town

library   library

**Read. Copy.**

the bank    _____

the town    _____

## Lesson **B** *Places around town*

☑ ■

**CIRCLE THE SAME.**   v  (v)  w  u  (v)(v)

v ___ V ___ W ___ U ___ V ___ V

j ___ J ___ g ___ J ___ g ___ j

**READ. TRACE. COPY.**

v ___ \ ___ V ___ V

j ___ j ___ j ___ j

**TRACE. READ. COPY.**

movie

jacket

**Lesson** **B** *Places around town*

**Trace. Read.**

MOVIE     movie

THEATER   theater

JACKET    jacket

**Read. Trace. Circle the same.**   movie   (movie)   move   (movie)

movie     movie        move         movie

theater   theater      theater      heater

jacket    jack         jacket       jacket

**Read. Trace. Copy.**

movie     movie _____

theater   theater _____

jacket    jacket _____

**Read. Copy.**

movie theater _____

57

# Lesson C It's on Main Street.

## TRACE. READ.

across from

next to

## READ. TRACE. CIRCLE THE SAME. across   cross ⟨across⟩

**across**   cross   across

**from**   from   form

**next**   next   nest

**to**   too   to

## TRACE. READ. COPY.

across from

next to

# Lesson C  *It's on Main Street.*

**Trace. Read.**

next to          across from

on               between

**Read. Circle.**

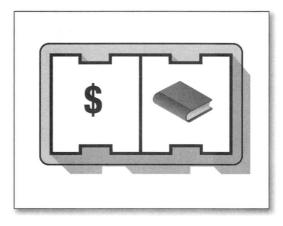

Where's the bank?

(Next to the library.)

Next to the post office.

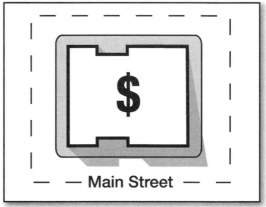

— Main Street —

Where's the bank?

On Fifth Street.

On Main Street.

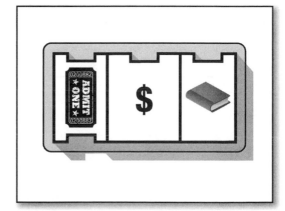

Where's the bank?

Across from the library.

Between the library
and the movie theater.

## TRACE. READ.

BUS bus    CAR car

BY by

## READ. TRACE. CIRCLE THE SAME.    bus (bus) bun (bus)

bus    bus bun bus

car    car ear car

by    by bye bye

## TRACE. READ. COPY.

by bus

by car

# Lesson **D** *Reading*

## Trace. Read. Circle the correct words.

(by bus)

by bus

by train

by car

by train

by car

## Write.

by train

## TRACE. READ.

ON          on

STREET   street

## READ. TRACE. COPY.

on          on

street     street

## TRACE. READ. COPY.

on Reed Street

on Main Street

## Trace. Read. Write.

restaurant | bank | library

Reed Street

post office | supermarket

The library is next to the ___bank___ .

The _____ is across from the post office.

The _____ is next to the post office.

The bank is between the _____ and the _____ .

The bank is on _____ _____ .

63

## TRACE. READ. COPY.

school

restaurant

library

hospital

post office

# Lesson F Another view

## Read. Trace. Copy.

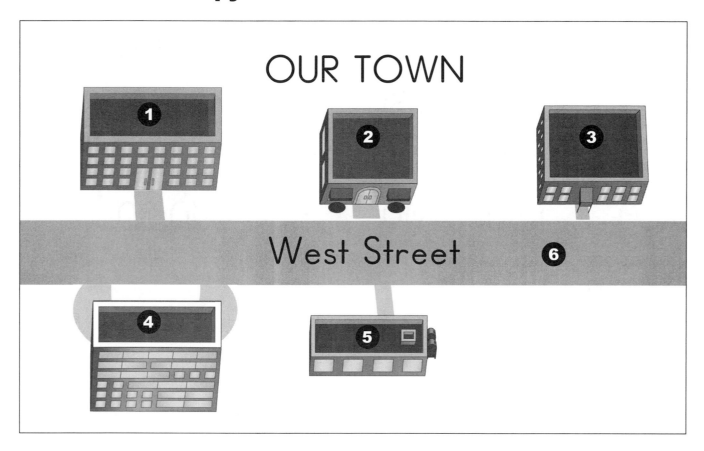

OUR TOWN

West Street

1. school

2. restaurant

3. library

4. hospital

5. post office

6. street

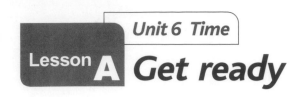

**Read. Circle the same.**  10:00  (10:00)  7:00  11:00  1:00

| 10:00 | 10:00 | 7:00 | 11:00 | 1:00 |
| 9:00 | 3:00 | 8:30 | 9:00 | 8:00 |
| 6:30 | 8:30 | 9:00 | 9:30 | 6:30 |
| 10:30 | 1:30 | 3:10 | 3:30 | 10:30 |

**Read. Trace. Copy.**

9:00   9:00 _____

10:00   10:00 _____

2:30   2:30 _____

6:30   6:30 _____

**Write the time.**

_____

# Lesson A Get ready

## Read. Trace. Copy.

9:00    9:00 _____

7:00    7:00 _____

10:30   10:30 _____

6:30    6:30 _____

## Write the time.

     7:00 _____

     _____

     _____

     _____

**Look. Trace.**

C c    C c    V v    V v

**Read. Circle** C **and** c. Ⓒ ⓒ    **Underline** V **and** v. V̲ v̲

CLASS    class    MOVIE    movie

**Read. Circle the same.**  CLASS  class  class  (CLASS)

| CLASS | class | class | CLASS |
| class | CLASS | CLASS | class |
| MOVIE | movie | movie | MOVIE |
| movie | MOVIE | movie | movie |

**Read. Trace. Copy.**

CLASS    CLASS _____

class    class _____

MOVIE    MOVIE _____

movie    movie _____

# Lesson **B** *Events*

## Read. Circle v.

m o v i e

## Write v. Read.

m o ___ i e

## Trace. Read.

class          movie          TV program

## Write.

class

## Lesson C *Is your class at 11:00?*

**Read. Circle the same.** class (class) lass (class) lass

| class | class | lass | class | lass |
|-------|-------|------|-------|------|
| is    | it    | is   | is    | it   |
| your  | your  | you  | your  | you  |
| at    | at    | as   | as    | at   |

**Read. Trace. Copy.**

Is your class at 11:00?

Is your class at 11:00?

_____

Yes, it is.

Yes, it is.

_____

No, it isn't.

No, it isn't.

_____

# Lesson C *Is your class at 11:00?*

**Read. Circle** Yes.    **Underline** No. <u>No</u>

Is your class at 12:00?

Yes, it is.

Is your movie at 8:00?

No, it isn't.

**Read. Write** it is **or** it isn't.

Is your party at 7:30?

No, _____it isn't_____ .

Is your meeting at 11:00?

Yes, _____ .

Is your class at 2:30?

No, _____ .

**Trace. Copy.**

Yes, it is.

No, it isn't.

## Look. Trace.

M m   M m   N n   N n

**Read. Circle** M **and** m. Ⓜ ⓜ   **Underline** N **and** n. N̲ n̲

MORNING   morning

**Read. Circle the same.**   MORNING   m̲o̲r̲n̲i̲n̲g̲   (MORNING)

MORNING   m̲o̲r̲n̲i̲n̲g̲   MORNING

morning   m̲o̲r̲n̲i̲n̲g̲   MORNING

## Read. Trace.

MORNING   MORNING   MORNING

morning   morning   morning

## Read. Copy.

MORNING   _____

morning   _____

## Lesson D Reading

**Read. Circle m.**

morning

**Write m. Read.**

___orning

**Read. Circle n.** (n)

evening

**Write n. Read.**

eve___i___g

**Trace. Read.**

8:00 a.m.    in the morning

8:00 p.m.    in the evening

**Read. Write.**

10:00 a.m.  in the morning _____

10:00 p.m.  in the evening _____

6:30 a.m.  _____

6:30 p.m.  _____

9:30 p.m.  _____

9:30 a.m.  _____

73

## Read. Circle the same.   a.m.   am   (a.m.)   m.a.   (a.m.)

a.m.   am   a.m.   m.a.   a.m.

p.m.   pm   p.m.   p.m.   m.p.

## Read. Trace. Copy.

8:00 a.m.   8:00 a.m. _____

8:00 p.m.   8:00 p.m. _____

1:00 a.m.   1:00 a.m. _____

1:00 p.m.   1:00 p.m. _____

## Read. Copy.

at 11:30 a.m.   _____

at 7:30 p.m.   _____

at 8:30 a.m.   _____

at 6:00 a.m.   _____

at 12:30 p.m.   _____

## Read. Trace. Write.

KIM'S TO-DO LIST

8:00 a.m. class

10:30 a.m. appointment

2:00 p.m. meeting

6:30 p.m. party

8:00 p.m. movie

Kim's _class_____ is at 8:00 _a.m._ .

Kim's _____ is at 10:30 _____ .

Kim's _____ is at 2:00 _____ .

Kim's _____ is at 6:30 _____ .

Kim's _____ is at 8:00 _____ .

**Circle** a.m.    **Underline** p.m. p.m.

| MORNING | AFTERNOON |
|---|---|
| 8:00 a.m. class | 1:30 p.m. meeting |
| 9:00 a.m. class | 3:00 p.m. appointment |
| 10:00 a.m. meeting | 5:00 p.m. party |

**Read. Trace. Write.**

APPOINTMENT
3:00 p.m.

Time: 3:00
in the afternoon

MEETING
10:00 a.m.

Time: _____
in the _____

PARTY
5:00 p.m.

Time: _____
in the _____

# Lesson F Another view

**Read. Circle. Copy.**

> ## JACKSON STREET ADULT SCHOOL PARTY!
>
> Thursday, July 12
> 2:00 p.m.
> Room 221
>
> 555-7018

The party is in the morning.

(The party is in the afternoon.)

The party is in the afternoon                    .

The party is at 2:00.

The party is at 12:00.

_____ .

The party is on Tuesday.

The party is on Thursday.

_____ .

**77**

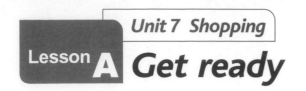

☑■

**Look. Trace.**

S s S s O o O o

**Read. Circle** S **and** s. Ⓢ Ⓢ **Underline** O **and** o. O̲ o̲

SOCKS socks SHOES shoes

**Read. Circle the same.** SOCKS socks (SOCKS) (SOCKS)

SOCKS socks SOCKS SOCKS

socks socks SOCKS socks

**Read. Trace.**

SOCKS SOCKS SOCKS SOCKS

socks socks socks socks

SHOES SHOES SHOES SHOES

shoes shoes shoes shoes

**Read. Copy.**

socks and shoes _____

## Lesson A *Get ready*

☑

**Read. Circle s.** ⓢ

s o c k s
s h o e s

**Write s. Read.**

__ o c k __
__ h o e __

**Trace. Read.**

socks    dress    shirt    shoes

**Write.**

shoes _____

_____

_____

_____

Lesson **B** *Clothing*

☑■

**Look. Trace.**

W  w    W  w

**Read. Circle** W **and** w.  Ⓦ ⓦ

SWEATER    sweater

**Read. Circle the same.**  SWEATER    sweater  (SWEATER)

SWEATER    sweater    SWEATER

sweater    sweater    SWEATER

**Read. Trace.**

SWEATER    SWEATER    SWEATER

sweater    sweater    sweater

**Read. Copy.**

SWEATER    _____

sweater    _____

### Read. Circle w. ⓦ

s w e a t e r

### Write w. Read.

s ___ e a t e r

### Trace. Read.

sweater      skirt      raincoat      blouse

### Write.

raincoat

_____      _____

# Lesson C How much are the shoes?

**Read. Circle the same.**  how  (how)  who  (how)  (how)

| how | how | who | how | how |
| much | munch | much | much | much |
| is | his | is | is | his |
| are | are | are | ear | are |

**Read. Trace. Copy.**

How much is the dress?

How much is the dress?

_____

How much are the socks?

How much are the socks?

_____

How much is the sweater?

How much is the sweater?

_____

# Lesson C  *How much are the shoes?*

**Read. Circle is.**   **Underline are.**  are

 How much is the blouse?

$19.99.

 How much are the socks?

$1.99.

**Read. Write is or are.**

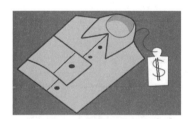 How much _____ the shirt?

$29.95.

 How much _____ the shoes?

$39.99.

 How much _____ the dress?

$18.00.

 How much _____ the sweater?

$17.95.

**Look. Trace.**

B b   B b   L l   L l

**Read. Circle** B **and** b. ⓑ ⓑ   **Underline** L **and** l. L̲ l̲

BLACK    black

BLUE     blue

BLOUSE   blouse

**Read. Circle the same.**   BLACK (BLACK) black (BLACK) black

BLACK   BLACK   black   BLACK   black

black   BLACK   black   black   black

**Read. Trace.**

BLACK   BLACK   BLACK   BLACK

black   black   black   black

**Read. Copy.**

BLACK   _____

black   _____

84

## Unit 7 Shopping

# Lesson D Reading

**Read. Circle b. ⓑ**

b l a c k
b l u e

**Write b. Read.**

__ l a c k
__ l u e

**Read. Circle l. ①**

b l a c k
b l u e

**Write l. Read.**

b __ a c k
b __ u e

**Trace. Read.**

black shoes        a black dress

blue socks        a blue blouse

**Write.**

 _____

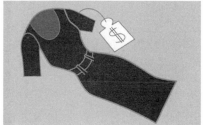 _____

**Read. Circle white.** (white) **Underline black.** black

a white blouse

a black skirt

black shoes

white socks

**Trace. Read. Copy.**

a white blouse _____

a black skirt _____

black shoes _____

white socks _____

**Read. Copy.**

a white skirt _____

a black blouse _____

black socks _____

white shoes _____

86

**Read. Trace. Write.**

Shopping List for Tina
- ✓ a blouse
- ✓ a skirt
- ✓ shoes

Shopping List for Jack
- ✓ a shirt
- ✓ a sweater
- ✓ socks

Tina needs a  blouse                    .

Tina needs a _____ .

Tina needs _____ .

Jack needs a _____ .

Jack needs a _____ .

Jack needs _____ .

**Trace. Read.**

TOTAL    total

**Read. Circle the same.**    TOTAL    total    (TOTAL) (TOTAL)

TOTAL    total    TOTAL    TOTAL

total    TOTAL    total    total

**Read. Trace. Copy.**

TOTAL    TOTAL _____

total    total _____

**Trace. Read.**

total    $6.95

total    $17.00

total    $23.99

TOTAL    $18.95

TOTAL    $2.80

TOTAL    $44.00

## Lesson F Another view

**Trace. Read. Circle TOTAL.** (TOTAL)

L-Mart
57 TOWN STREET
BOSTON, MA 02101

| blouse | 12.95 |
|--------|-------|
| shoes | 24.00 |
| sweater | 18.95 |
| Subtotal | 55.90 |
| Tax | 2.80 |
| TOTAL | $58.70 |

Thank you for shopping at L-Mart.
Have a nice day! ☺

**Read. Write.**

The blouse is $ 1 2 . 9 5 .

The shoes are $ __ __ . __ __ .

The sweater is $ __ __ . __ __ .

The total is $ __ __ . __ __ .

**Look. Trace.**

E e  E e    H h  H h

**Read. Circle** E **and** e. Ⓔ ⓔ   **Underline** H **and** h. H h

MECHANIC    mechanic

**Read. Circle the same.**  MECHANIC   mechanic  (MECHANIC)

MECHANIC    mechanic    MECHANIC

mechanic    mechanic    MECHANIC

**Read. Trace.**

MECHANIC    MECHANIC

mechanic    mechanic

**Read. Copy.**

MECHANIC    _____

mechanic    _____

**Read. Circle** e. ⓔ

m e c h a n i c

**Write** e. **Read.**

m __ c h a n i c

**Read. Circle** h. ⓗ

c a s h i e r

**Write** h. **Read.**

c a s __ i e r

**Trace. Read.**

mechanic          cashier          receptionist

**Write.**

mechanic

☑■

**Look. Trace.**

F f    F f    T t    T t

**Read. Circle** T **and** t. (T)(t)    **Underline** F **and** f. F f

COUNT    count    FIX    fix

**Read. Circle the same.**    COUNT    (COUNT)    count    (COUNT)

| COUNT | COUNT | count | COUNT |
|-------|-------|-------|-------|
| count | count | COUNT | count |
| FIX | FIX | fix | FIX |
| fix | FIX | fix | fix |

**Read. Trace. Copy.**

COUNT    COUNT _____

count    count _____

FIX    FIX _____

fix    fix _____

92

## Read. Circle t. (t)

count
first

## Write t. Read.

coun___
firs___

## Read. Circle f. (f)

fix
first

## Write f. Read.

___ix
___irst

## Trace. Read.

counts money      fixes cars      serves food

## Write.

_____

_____

**Read. Circle the same.** yes (yes) year yen

| yes | yes | year | yen |
| no | an | no | on |
| does | do | dose | does |
| doesn't | don't | donut | doesn't |

**Trace. Read.**

Does he fix cars?

No, he doesn't.

Does he count money?

Yes, he does.

# Lesson C Does he sell clothes?

## Read. Circle.

Does she count money?

(Yes, she does.)

No, she doesn't.

Does he fix cars?

Yes, he does.

No, he doesn't.

## Write.

Does she fix cars?

_____ .

Does he serve food?

_____ .

**Look. Trace.**

K k    K k    U u    U u

**Read. Circle** K **and** k. Ⓚ Ⓚ    **Underline** U **and** u. U̲ u̲

TRUCK      truck

**Read. Circle the same.**   TRUCK   t̲r̲u̲c̲k̲   ⟨TRUCK⟩ ⟨TRUCK⟩

TRUCK    t̲r̲u̲c̲k̲    TRUCK    TRUCK

truck    T̲R̲U̲C̲K̲    truck    TRUCK

**Read. Trace.**

TRUCK    TRUCK   TRUCK   TRUCK

truck    truck    truck    truck

**Read. Copy.**

TRUCK      _____

truck      _____

# Lesson D Reading

**Read. Circle k.** (k)

truck
desk

**Write k. Read.**

truc___
des___

**Read. Circle u.** (u)

truck
bus

**Write u. Read.**

tr___ck
b___s

**Trace. Read.**

bus driver        truck driver

**Read. Trace. Write.**

What does he do?

He's a _____.

What does she do?

She's a _____.

**Read. Circle** truck.  **Underline** bus. <u>bus</u>

a truck driver

a bus driver

**Trace. Read.**

a truck driver    a truck driver

a bus driver      a bus driver

**Write.**

_____

_____

## Read. Circle. Copy.

His name is Tim.

His name is Jim.

_____ .

He is a mechanic.

He is a bus driver.

_____ .

He drives a bus.

He fixes cars.

_____ .

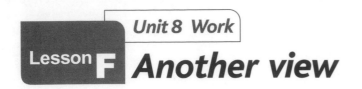

**Read.**

JOB
_____

CASHIER

$9.00 an hour

Saturday and Sunday

ABC Store

**Read. Trace. Copy.**

cashier    cashier _____

an hour    an hour _____

**Read. Trace.**

$9.00 an hour    $9.00 an hour _____

**Read. Copy.**

$9.00 an hour    _____

**Read. Trace.**

> HELP WANTED: CASHIER
> _____
> $9.00 an hour
> Saturday and Sunday
> ABC Store      555-1289

The job is for a _____cashier_____ .

The job is $9.00 an _____hour_____ .

The phone number is _____555-1289_____ .

**Read. Write.**

> JOB: CUSTODIAN
> _____
> $8.50 an hour
> Saturday
> 6:00 to 3:00
> Arbor Library      555-4273

The job is for a _____ .

The job is _____ .

The phone number is _____ .

**Look. Trace.**

I i   I i

**Read. Circle I and i.** I i

WASHING   washing   DISHES   dishes

**Read. Circle the same.**   WASHING   WASHING   washing

| WASHING | WASHING | washing |
|---------|---------|---------|
| washing | WASHING | washing |
| DISHES  | dishes  | DISHES  |
| dishes  | DISHES  | dishes  |

**Read. Trace. Copy.**

| DISHES  | DISHES  |
|---------|---------|
| dishes  | dishes  |
| WASHING | WASHING |
| washing | washing |

**Lesson A Get ready**

**Read. Circle i.** (i)

washing
dishes

**Write i. Read.**

wash___ng
d___shes

**Trace. Read.**

washing the dishes    drying the dishes

making lunch

**Write.**

_____

_____

_____

**Look. Trace.**

G g    G g    A a    A a

**Read. Circle** G **and** g. (G)(g)    **Underline** A **and** a. <u>A</u> <u>a</u>

GRASS    grass      TRASH    trash

**Read. Circle the same.**   GRASS (GRASS) grass (GRASS)

| GRASS | GRASS | grass | GRASS |
|-------|-------|-------|-------|
| grass | grass | grass | GRASS |
| TRASH | TRASH | trash | TRASH |
| trash | trash | TRASH | trash |

**Read. Trace. Copy.**

| GRASS | GRASS |
|-------|-------|
| grass | grass |
| TRASH | TRASH |
| trash | trash |

# Lesson **B** *Outside chores*

**Read. Circle g.** (g)

g r a s s
g e t

**Write g. Read.**

___ r a s s
___ e t

**Read. Circle a.** (a)

g r a s s
t r a s h

**Write a. Read.**

g r ___ s s
t r ___ s h

**Trace. Read.**

cutting the grass      getting the mail

taking out the trash

**Write.**

_____

_____

## Lesson **C** *What are they doing?*

**Read. Circle the same.**  what   who  (what)  hat  (what)

| what | who | what | hat | what |
|------|-----|------|-----|------|

| doing | doing | ding | doing | do |
|-------|-------|------|-------|-----|

**Read. Trace. Copy.**

What is she doing?

Making lunch.

_____

What is he doing?

Making the bed.

_____

**Lesson C** *What are they doing?*

**Read. Circle** Making. (Making)

What is he doing?

Making lunch.

What is she doing?

Making the bed.

**Write.**

What is she doing?

_____ .

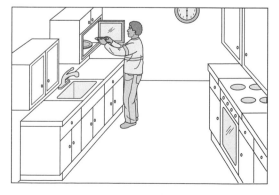

What is he doing?

_____ .

**Look. Trace.**

R r  R r  D d  D d

**Read. Circle** R **and** r.   **Underline** D **and** d. D d

ROOM        room

BEDROOM     bedroom

**Read. Circle the same.**  BEDROOM (BEDROOM) bedroom

BEDROOM     BEDROOM     bedroom

bedroom     bedroom     BEDROOM

**Read. Trace.**

BEDROOM     BEDROOM   BEDROOM

bedroom     bedroom     bedroom

**Read. Copy.**

BEDROOM     _____

bedroom     _____

# Lesson D Reading

**Read. Circle r.**

b e d r o o m
b a t h r o o m

**Write r. Read.**

b e d __ o o m
b a t h __ o o m

**Read. Circle d.** d

b e d r o o m
d i n i n g   r o o m

**Write d. Read.**

b e __ r o o m
__ i n i n g   r o o m

**Trace. Read.**

the bedroom    the bathroom    the dining room

**Read. Trace. Write.**

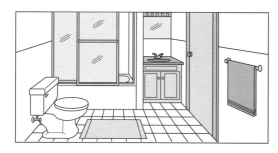

What room is this?

The _____ .

What room is this?

The _____ .

☑■

**Read. Trace.**

| washing | *washing* | *washing* |
| taking out | *taking out* | *taking out* |
| the car | *the car* | *the car* |
| the trash | *the trash* | *the trash* |
| the dishes | *the dishes* | *the dishes* |

**Read. Trace. Copy.**

washing the car

*washing the car*

_____

taking out the trash

*taking out the trash*

_____

_____

washing the dishes

*washing the dishes*

_____

_____

## Read. Circle.

What is Sam doing?

Washing the dishes.

(Washing the car.)

What is Carla doing?

Taking out the trash.

Getting the mail.

## Read. Write.

What is Sam doing?

_____ .

What is Carla doing?

_____ .

**Read.**

| Chore | Mom | Dad |
|---|---|---|
| walk the dog | ✓ | |
| water the grass | | ✓ |
| wash the dishes | ✓ | |
| wash the car | | ✓ |

**Trace. Copy.**

Mom:  <u>walk the dog</u>

_____

<u>wash the dishes</u>

_____

Dad:  <u>water the grass</u>

_____

<u>wash the car</u>

_____

## Lesson F  Another view

**Read. Trace. Write.**

Home Cleaning Service

Date: April 28
Work Order for: 410 South Main Street

| Name | Chore |
|------|-------|
| Eva | water the grass |
| Don | walk the dog |
| Kay | wash the car |

Eva is _watering_____ .

Don is _____ .

Kay is _____ .

**Look. Trace.**

P p   P p   AY ay   AY ay

**Read. Circle** P **and** p. P p   **Underline** AY **and** ay. AY ay

PLAY   play

**Read. Circle the same.** PLAY (PLAY) play (PLAY)(PLAY)

PLAY   PLAY   play   PLAY   PLAY

play   play   PLAY   play   play

**Read. Trace.**

PLAY   PLAY   PLAY   PLAY   PLAY

play   play   play   play   play

**Read. Copy.**

PLAY   _____

play   _____

# Lesson A *Get ready*

## Read. Circle ay. (ay)

p l a y
d a y

## Write ay. Read.

p l __ __
d __ __

## Trace. Read.

play basketball    play cards    dance

## Write.

_____

_____

_____

**Look. Trace.**

CH ch    CH ch

**Read. Circle CH and ch.** CH ch

WATCH    watch

**Read. Circle the same.** WATCH   watch   WATCH   watch

WATCH    watch    WATCH    watch

watch    watch    WATCH    WATCH

**Read. Trace.**

WATCH    WATCH    WATCH    WATCH

watch    watch    watch    watch

**Read. Copy.**

WATCH    _____

watch    _____

# Lesson B *Around the house*

## Read. Circle ch. (ch)

w a t c h
c h a i r
m u c h

## Write ch. Read.

w a t __ __

__ __ a i r

m u __ __

## Trace. Read.

listen to music     watch TV     play the guitar

## Write.

_____

_____

_____

**117**

## Lesson C  *I like to swim.*

**Read. Circle the same.**   like to  (like to)  bike to  lie to

| like to | like to | bike to | lie to |
| like to | *like to* | *bike to* | *lie to* |
| likes to | *bikes to* | *likes to* | *lies to* |
| swim | *swim* | *wins* | *swims* |

**Read. Trace. Copy.**

They like to swim.

They like to swim .

_____ .

He likes to swim.

He likes to swim .

_____ .

Lesson **C** *I like to swim.*

## Read. Circle.

What does she like to do?

   She likes to play cards.

   (She likes to swim.)

What do they like to do?

   They like to watch TV.

   They like to listen to music.

## Read. Write.

What does she like to do?

She likes to _____ .

What do they like to do?

They like to _____ .

**Look. Trace.**

SH sh     SH sh

**Read. Circle SH and sh.** SH sh

SHOP    shop
FISH    fish

**Read. Circle the same.** SHOP    shop (SHOP) shop

SHOP    shop      SHOP    shop

shop    SHOP    shop    SHOP

**Read. Trace.**

SHOP    SHOP    SHOP    SHOP    SHOP
shop    shop    shop    shop    shop

**Read. Copy.**

SHOP    _____

shop    _____

# Lesson D Reading

**Read. Circle sh.** (sh)

s h o p
f i s h
d i s h e s

**Write sh. Read.**

__ __ o p
f i __ __
d i __ __ e s

**Trace. Read.**

shop    go to the movies    visit friends

**Read. Write.**

What does she like to do?

She likes to _____ .

What does he like to do?

He likes to _____ .

What do they like to do?

They like to _____ .

**121**

**Read. Circle the same.**   exercise    ~~excise~~ (exercise)(exercise)

| exercise | excise | exercise | exercise |
|----------|--------|----------|----------|
| cook | cook | cork | cook |
| dance | lance | dance | dance |

**Read. Trace. Copy.**

| exercise | exercise |
|----------|----------|
| cook | cook |
| dance | dance |

**Trace. Read.**

She likes to exercise .

He likes to cook      .

They like to dance   .

He likes to exercise  .

They like to cook    .

## Lesson E Writing

**Read. Circle.**

What does she like to do?

She likes to exercise.

She likes to cook.

What does he like to do?

He likes to cook.

He likes to swim.

**Trace. Read.**

exercise    cook    dance    swim

**Write.**

What does he like to do?

He likes to _____ .

What does she like to do?

She likes to _____ .

**Read.**

DANCE CLASS
Learn to dance!
Saturday, October 3
9:00 a.m. to 12:00 p.m.
$25.00

**Read. Trace.**

dance    dance    dance    dance    dance

class    class    class    class    class

**Read. Copy.**

dance class _____

**Trace. Read. Copy.**

The dance class is on Saturday.

_____

## Read. Trace.

Guitar Class     $100.00
Monday, September 1, 8, 15, 22, and 29
9:00 a.m. to 12:00 p.m.     Room A

This is for a _____guitar_____ class.

The class is $ _____100.00_____ .

The class is on _____Monday_____ .

## Read. Write.

Dance Class     $75.00
Saturday, April 3
8:00 a.m. to 4:00 p.m.

This is for a _____ class.

The class is $ _____ .

The class is on _____ .

# Extra practice

## Welcome unit

0 0 0 0

1 1 1 1

2 2 2 2

3 3 3 3

4 4 4 4

5 5 5 5

6 6 6 6

7 7 7 7

8 8 8 8

9 9 9 9

# Unit 1

I I I I

H H H H

E E E E

J J J J

G G G G

V V V V

# Unit 2

A A A A A

N N N N N

M M M M M

S S S S

P P P P

R R R R

D D D D

B B B B

K K K K

Y Y Y Y

W W W W

# Unit 3

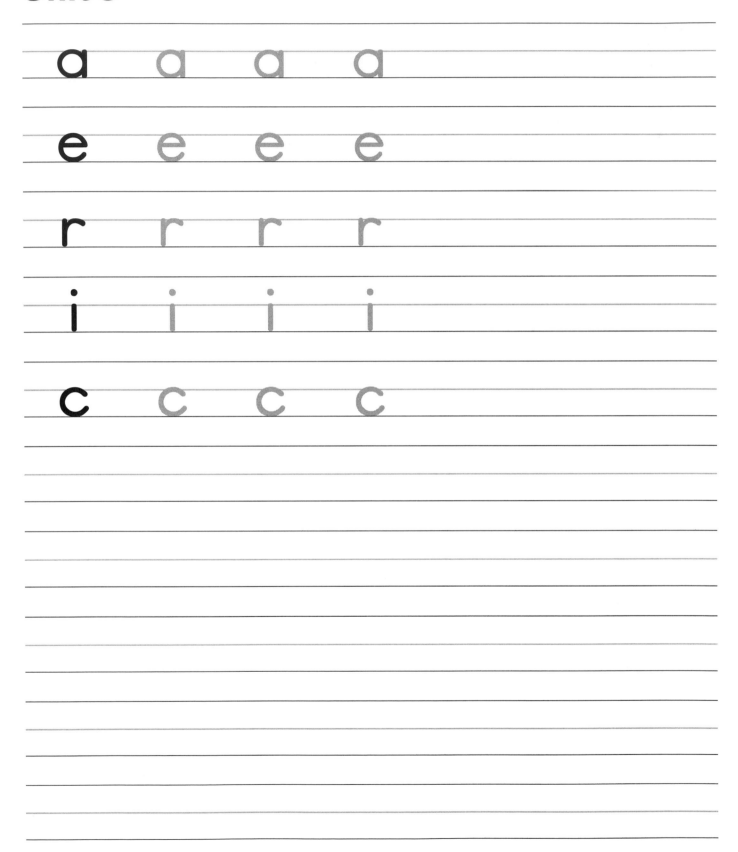

a    a    a    a

e    e    e    e

r    r    r    r

i    i    i    i

c    c    c    c

u   u   u   u

d   d   d   d

b   b   b   b

h   h   h   h

# Unit 4

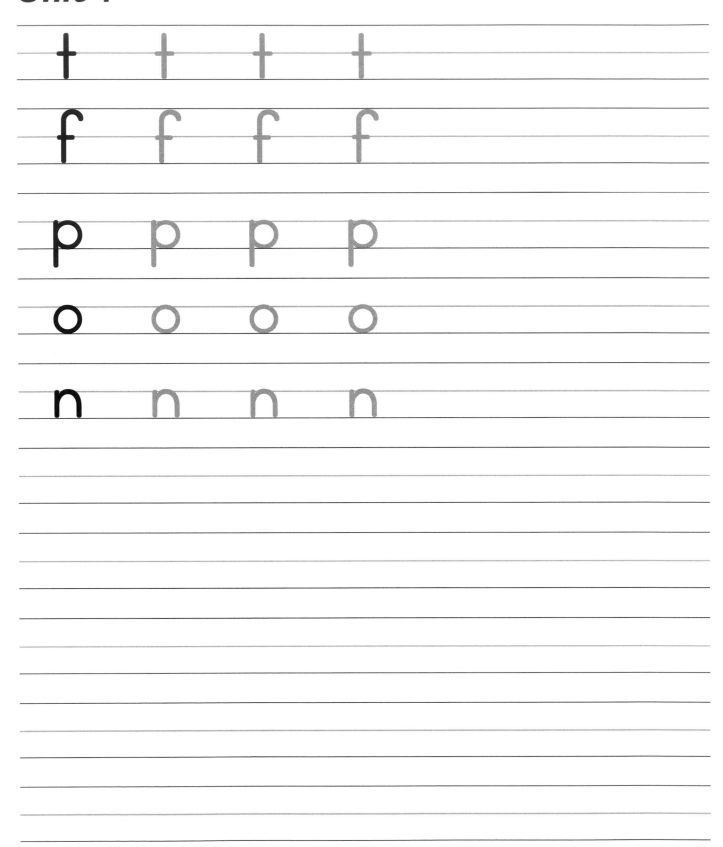

t t t t

f f f f

p p p p

o o o o

n n n n

m m m m

s s s s

l l l l

g g g g

# Unit 5

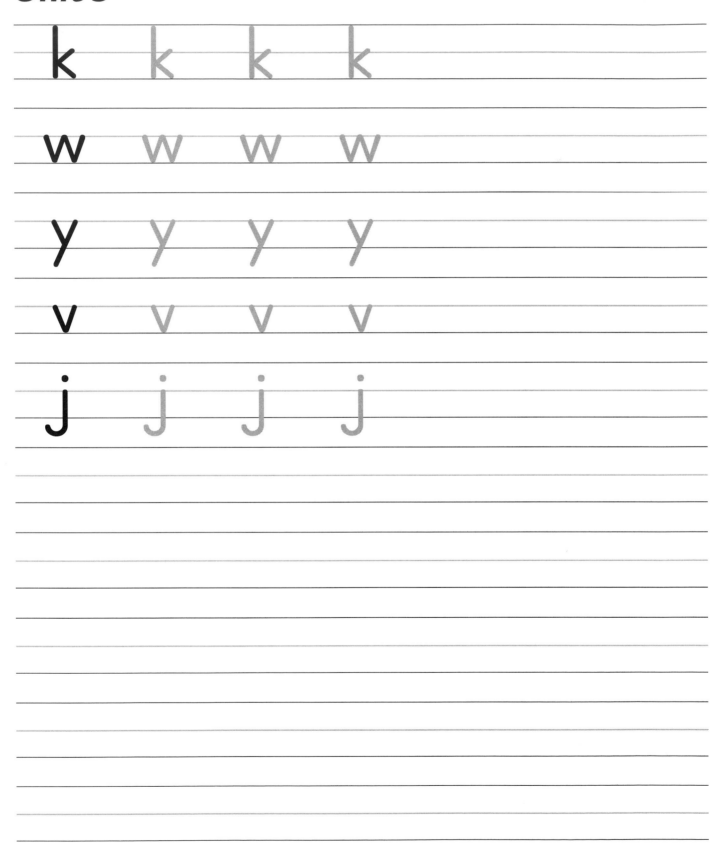

k k k k

w w w w

y y y y

v v v v

j j j j

# Unit 6

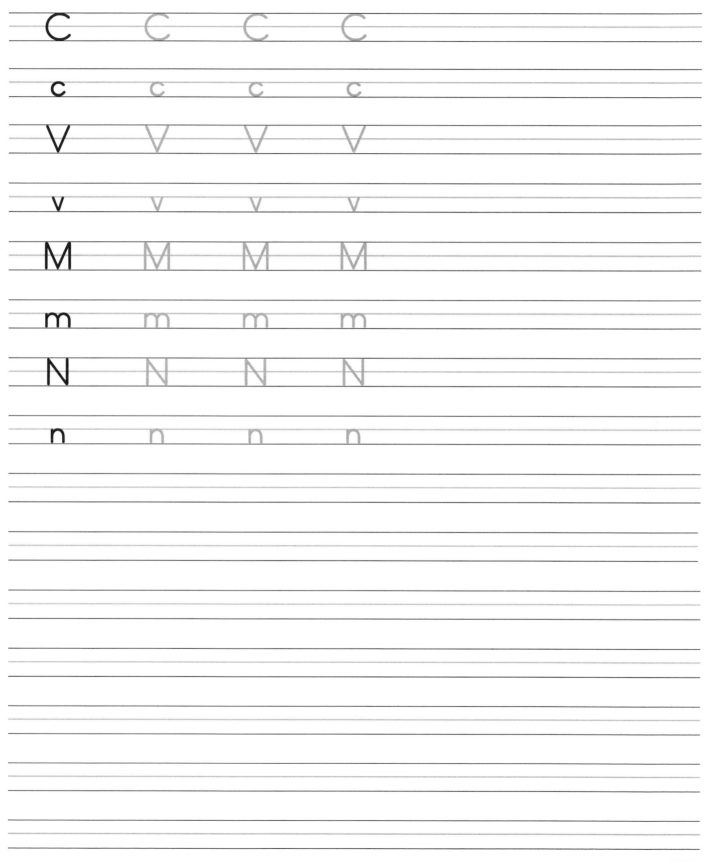

C C C C

c c c c

V V V V

v v v v

M M M M

m m m m

N N N N

n n n n

# Unit 7

S    S    S    S

s    s    s    s

O    O    O    O

o    o    o    o

W    W    W    W

w    w    w    w

B    B    B    B

b    b    b    b

L    L    L    L

l    l    l    l

# Unit 8

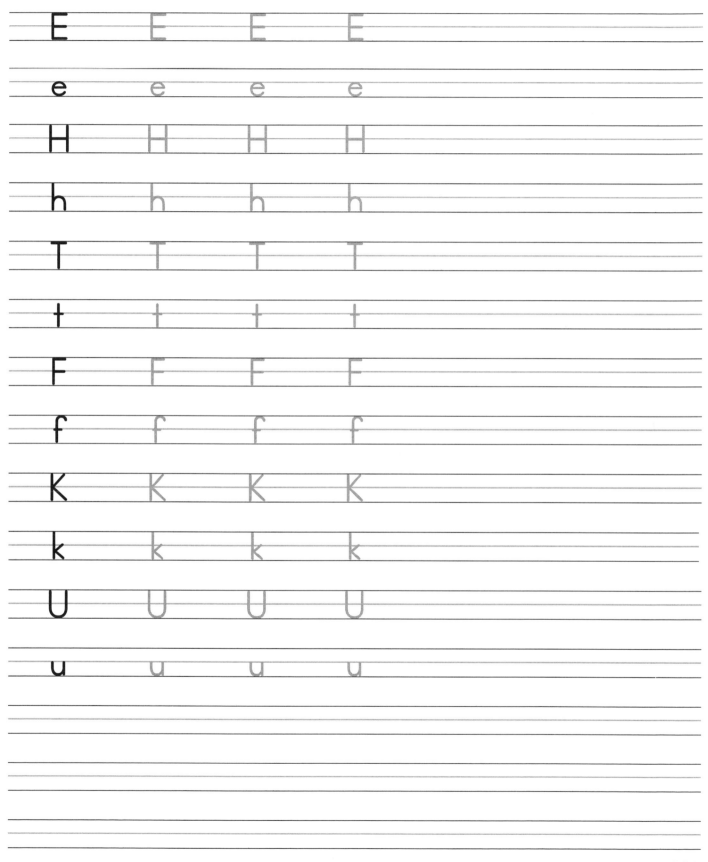

E E E E

e e e e

H H H H

h h h h

T T T T

t t t t

F F F F

f f f f

K K K K

k k k k

U U U U

u u u u

# Unit 9

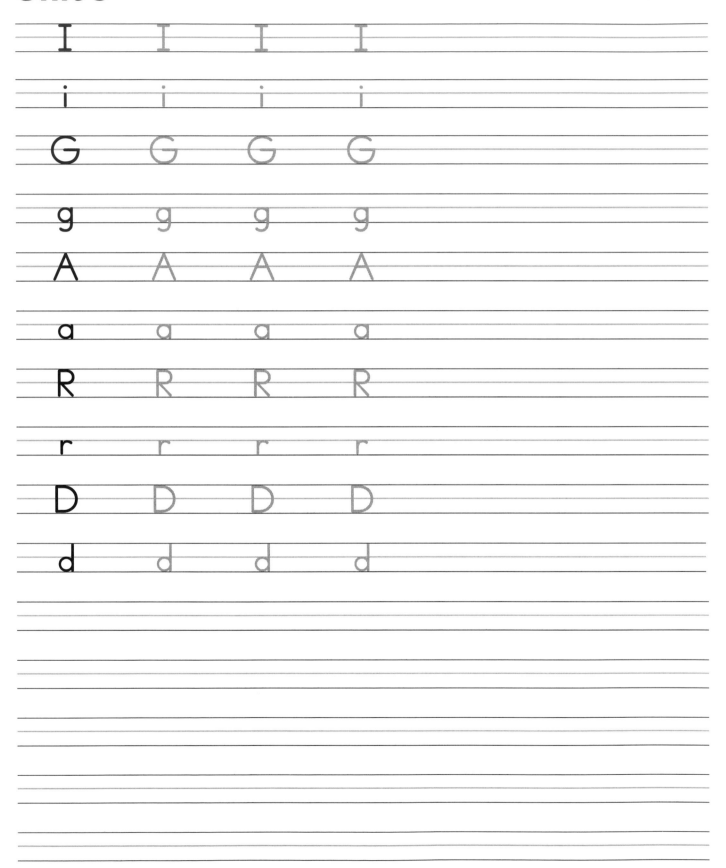

I   I   I   I

i   i   i   i

G   G   G   G

g   g   g   g

A   A   A   A

a   a   a   a

R   R   R   R

r   r   r   r

D   D   D   D

d   d   d   d

# Unit 10

P  P  P  P

p  p  p  p

AY  AY  AY  AY

ay  ay  ay  ay

CH  CH  CH  CH

ch  ch  ch  ch

SH  SH  SH  SH

sh  sh  sh  sh

# Additional letters

X X X X

x x x x

Z Z Z Z

z z z z

Q Q Q Q

q q q q

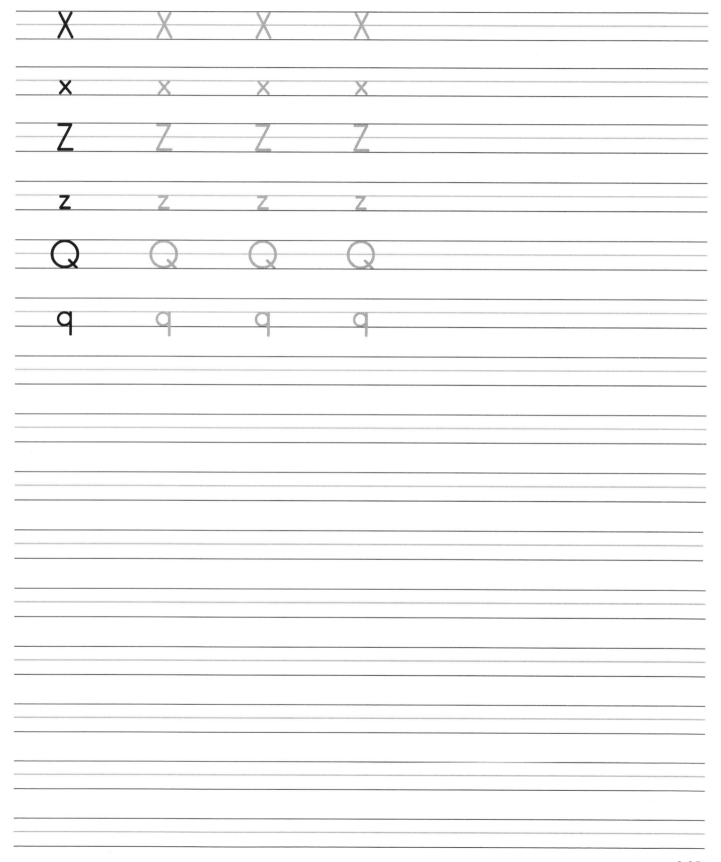

# Letters and numbers

A B C D E F G

H I J K L M N

O P Q R S T U

V W X Y Z

a b c d e f g

h i j k l m n

o p q r s t u

v w x y z

0 1 2 3 4 5 6

7 8 9

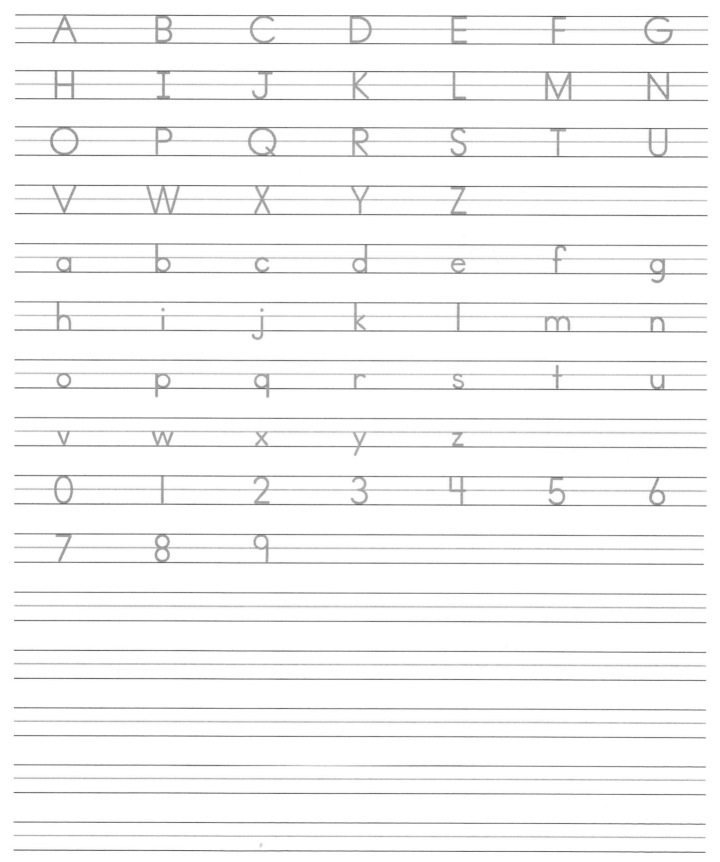